An Explanation of
Excel 2007

Barb Henderson

Order this book online at www.trafford.com
or email orders@trafford.com

Most Trafford titles are also available at major online book retailers.

Note for Librarians: A cataloguing record for this book is available from Library and Archives Canada at www.collectionscanada.ca/amicus/index-e.html

Printed in Victoria, BC, Canada.

ISBN: 978-1-4269-1054-8 (soft)
ISBN: 978-1-4269-1055-5 (hard)
ISBN: 978-1-4269-1056-2 (ebook)

We at Trafford believe that it is the responsibility of us all, as both individuals and corporations, to make choices that are environmentally and socially sound. You, in turn, are supporting this responsible conduct each time you purchase a Trafford book, or make use of our publishing services. To find out how you are helping, please visit www.trafford.com/responsiblepublishing.html

Our mission is to efficiently provide the world's finest, most comprehensive book publishing service, enabling every author to experience success. To find out how to publish your book, your way, and have it available worldwide, visit us online at www.trafford.com

Trafford rev. 7/2/2009

 www.trafford.com

North America & international
toll-free: 1 888 232 4444 (USA & Canada)
phone: 250 383 6864 ♦ fax: 250 383 6804 ♦ email: info@trafford.com

Contents

3   Contents

Getting Started

Excel is a useful tool for calculations and data management. Whether you are familiar with earlier versions of Excel or are just starting out with Excel this manual will show you the features and abilities of the program.

The screen for Excel 2007 looks quite different than previous versions.

All screens

The descriptions that follow are common to all screens in the Excel work book.

The Office Button

- On the top left of the screen you will notice the office button. This button will lead a number of commands.

- Click on the Office Button [image].
- The options that are displayed in the menu are similar to the options that were available under the file option in previous versions.
- These option include **New, Open and Save** and **Save As**.
- The **New** command will open a new Excel spreadsheet.
- The **Open** command will produce a list previous documents that have been saved.
- The **Save** command allows you to save the changes that you have made to your documents.

- The **Save As** command allows you to save the document with a different name.
- The next set of options will allow you to produce the document. They include **Print, Prepare, Send** and **Publish**.
  - The **Print** provides you with three options: Print, Quick Print and Print Preview.
    - **Print** will display a dialogue box allowing you to select options regarding the printing of this document.
    - **Quick Print** does just that. It sends the document to the default printer in the default format.
    - **Print Preview** allows you to see your document as it will look when it is printed.
  - **Prepare** will prepare the document for distribution.
    - **Properties** – Allows you to view and edit document properties.
    - **Inspect Document** –Checks your document for a number of properties that you are able to select from a dialogue box.
    - **Encrypt Document** asks you for a password and when you supply the password will make the file unreadable to anyone opening the document unless they can enter the correct password.
    - **Add digital Signature** is a method of verifying your identity. There are two methods of creating a digital signature.
    - The first method is to create your own. This method has limited abilities in verifying your identity.
    - The second method is to access Microsoft partners who will charge for the purchase of the digital signature.

    - **Mark as Final** will mark the document as final and save it as read only.

- **Run Compatibility Checker** will check for issues regarding earlier versions of Excel opening and using this document.
- **Send** allows you to send your document by two different methods.
  - **Email**-you can send an email with this document as an attachment.
  - **Fax** –you are able to fax this document.
- **Publish** enables your document to be worked on by more than one person
  - **Document Management Server** will open up access to your network places so that it can be accessed by other individuals on your network.
  - **Create Document Workspace** is designed to work with a Microsoft SharePoint. If you have access to a SharePoint workspace site then a copy made on the SharePoint and will be synchronized with your copy.
- **Close** closes the document.

Quick Access Toolbar

- At the top left side of the Excel screen is the **Quick Access Toolbar** this toolbar will appear on every screen. These are functions that you will use frequently. The standard functions are: **Save, Undo** and **Redo**.
  - There is also a list arrow on this bar. Clicking this will return the following menu.

- The items that are checked currently appear on the **Quick Access Toolbar.** This menu allows you to select other options to appear on you **Quick Access Toolbar**.
- In addition to the items listed there is a More **Commands**.
- Clicking this will return unlimited number of commands that you may add to this toolbar.
- The menus are divided into subheadings with a completely new set of options on each one.

The ribbon

- Under each tab heading there is a ribbon of commands.
- On each ribbon there are categories of commands organized with the title of the commands below.

- For example, on the **Home** menu, we have the category of Font. This category has commands such as font size, font colour and font type.
- On the bottom right hand corner of some categories, we find an arrow. Clicking this arrow will produce a dialogue box. The dialogue box will allow you to access additional font commands.

In this instance the arrow will show the font tab of the Format cells dialogue box.

Name Box and Formula Bar

Below the ribbon on all screens is the row that contains the name box and the formula bar.

Name Box

- The name box identifies where your cursor is situated. From the illustration above, the cursor is located at cell A1.
- You are able to move to specific cells using the name box.
- For Example, select the A1, key in Z99 and press enter.

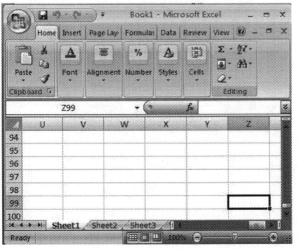

- Your cursor is moved to that exact location on your worksheet.
- A more effective way to move might be to name the range of cells that you would like to access.
- Select a range of cells. Click to highlight the value in the name box. Key in Summer_Sales and press enter. There can be no spaces and no punctuation in the name.
- You have named this range of cells.

	A	B	C	D
1				
2		July	$562	
3		August	$674	
4		September	$789	

- Move to another location on your worksheet.

- To access the named range of cells click the list arrow to the right of the name box.

- Select Summer_Sales from the drop-down list and press enter. The Summer_Sales will be highlighted again.

Formula Bar

The **Formula Bar** is located to the right of the Name Box, below the ribbon on each page.

- The Formula bar shows what data is contained in the selected cell.
- The Formula Bar is where you are able to create formulas in Excel.

- Below is a list of operators used in creating formulas in Excel.

Excel Operator Symbols	
Plus	+
Minus	-
Multiply	*
Divide	/

- For example, we will create a formula to add two numbers.
- Select the cell where you would like the result to appear.
- Every formula in excel begins with an equal sign.
- Key in an equal sign and select a value from your worksheet, key in a plus sign and select another value from your worksheet.

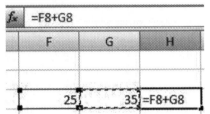

- To calculate the formula press enter.

Insert Functions

- The insert Function dialogue box is also available from the formula bar.
- The insert function dialogue box will guide you through more advanced steps and functions.
- Select the cell where you would like to have your result appear.
- Click the Fx.
- The Insert Function dialogue box will be presented.

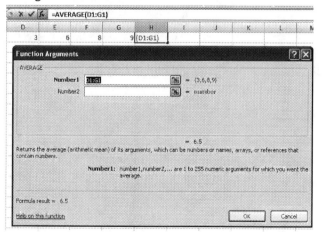

- If, for example, we are going to use the average function we would select the cell where we would like to have the average displayed normally it would be close to the numbers that we want to average.
- Click the Fx on the formula bar and select average from the dialogue box and click O.K.

- Excel will suggest which numbers you want to average. If what they have suggested is correct click O.K. to calculate.
- If Excel's suggestion is incorrect delete the fields that Excel has in the Number1 field and click the button at the end of the

number field  to go back to the worksheet and select the correct cells.

View Options

- On the bottom right of all excel screens you will find the view options.

```
▦ ▣ ▥   100%  ⊖
```

- These options are normal, page layout and page break preview.
- The **Normal** is the default view which is your normal working view.
- **Page Layout** is a view of how the page will look when it is printed.
- The **Page Break** preview will allow you to modify where the pages will break.

	A	B	C	D	E	F	G	H	I	J
1										
2										
3		Monday	1	2	3	4	5	6	7	8
4		Tuesday	1	2	3	4	5	6	7	8
5		Wednes	1	2	3	4	5	6	7	8
6		Thursda	1	2	3	4	5	6	7	8
7		Friday	1	2	3	4	5	6	7	8
8		Saturda	1	2	3	4	5	6	7	8
9		Sunday	1	2	3	4	5	6	7	8
10		Monday	1	2	3	4	5	6	7	8
11		Tuesday	1	2	3	4	5	6	7	8
12		Wednes	1	2	3	4	5	6	7	8
13		Thursda	1	2	3	4	5	6	7	8
14		Friday	1	2	3	4	5	6	7	8
15		Saturda	1	2	3	4	5	6	7	8

- As seen from the graphic above, the page break is indicated by the dashed line in page break preview. You are able to place your cursor over the dashed line and drag to another location.
- In this case, your page break will be located including the J column.

- Next to the View options is a zoom bar. The 100% indicates that you are viewing the page at normal size. Clicking the plus or minus sign will change this view.
- Clicking on the 100% will bring up a zoom toolbar which you are able to select the zoom percentage that you require.

Splitting the Sheet

Splitting an Excel sheet will allow you to view the top and bottom of a long sheet at the same time.

- Place your cursor over the bar on the right hand side directly below the formula bar.

- Click and hold the click and drag down several rows on your sheet.
- If you scroll down on the bottom section of your worksheet, you will still be able to see what is on the top of the sheet.

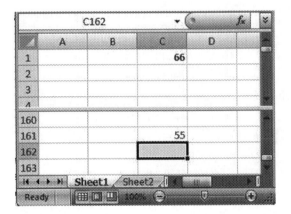

- From the graphic above, we are able to view in column C lines 1 and 161.
- To remove the split drag the dividing bar back toward the formula bar.

Sheet Tabs

- On the bottom of the page are sheet tabs.
- The reason that excel files are referred to as books is due to the fact that they are a combination of a number of sheets.

- The sheet tabs are names **Sheet1**, **Sheet 2**, etc.
- Right clicking on the sheet tabs, will allow you to access a number of commands.

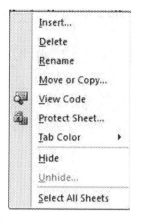

- o **Insert** – inserts a new worksheet.
- o **Delete**- deletes selected worksheet.
- o **Rename**-Allows you to rename the current sheet.
- o **Move or Copy** – Allows you to move or copy.
- o **View Code**- You are able to view the visual basic code for this worksheet.
- o **Protect Sheet**-You are able to set up password protection to view or change worksheet.
- o **Tab Colour**-Allows you to select a background colour for the sheet tab.
- o **Hide/Unhide** –You are able to hide or unhide.
- o **Select All Sheets**- Enables the selection of all sheets.

The Cells
The worksheets of Excel are made up of cells. The columns are named by letters and the rows are numbered. Therefore cell D5 would be the cell that was in the fourth column and the fifth row.

Movement
- Click the **Tab** key on your keyboard to advance horizontally.

- Press **Enter** or **Return** key on your keyboard to move vertically.
- You are able to move to any cell by clicking on it with your mouse.

Data

- Data of any kind may be entered in each cell
- Numbers, values that can be used in a formula are by default aligned to the right.
- Labels, words, letters or heading numbers are formatted to the left.
- Formulas begin with an equal sign.
- If you have a number as a label, before the number is typed, key in ' .

Fill Handle

- There is a feature to aid in data entry.
- When you click on a cell there is a small box at the bottom right hand side of the cell known as the fill handle.

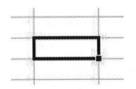

- When your mouse pointer is placed over the fill handle the pointer becomes a thin plus sign **+.**
- For example, if you key in **Monday**, place the mouse pointer over the little box, Fill handle, until it becomes a plus sign. Next, click and hold the click and drag the mouse to the right.

| Monday | Tuesday | Wednesday | Thursday |

- The next day names will be auto populated
- This function works for days of the week or months of the year dragging horizontally or vertically.
- The Fill Handle will also extend number lists.
- Key in the numbers 3 and 6.

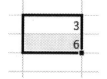

- Select the two numbers and click and drag the fill handle downward for two cells.
- The numbers will be extended in the same sequence.

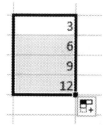

- You are also able to extend formulas. For example, if you are multiplying the numbers in two colunms, complete the formula in the first row and select the fill handle for cell with the formula in and drag down.

B	C	D	E
	hours	wages	
joe	35	$ 21.00	=C4*D4
brenda	22	$ 23.00	
lisa	37	$ 16.00	
Henry	40	$ 22.00	

- The formula will now fill all the rows.

B	C	D	E
	hours	wages	
joe	35	$ 21.00	$ 735.00
brenda	22	$ 23.00	$ 506.00
lisa	37	$ 16.00	$ 592.00
Henry	40	$ 22.00	$ 880.00

Absolute and Relative Cell Reference

- When creating a formula, when you are calculating two columns of numbers you are able to drag the formula down.

- This procedure only works when both values are located relative to each other's position, Relative Cell Reference.

- When, however, you would like to calculate a column of numbers by using only one value, this is referred to as Absolute Cell Reference.

- After selecting the number that will remain the same in the formula, click the F4 button on your keyboard. This will put $ in front of column and the row number of the cell reference.

- The $ will inform Excel that when you drag the formula down, this value will remain the same.

- In the example we will calculate the holiday pay for each of the staff. The holiday pay is at a rate of 5% indicated in cell F2.

- Select E4 multiplied by F2. Click the F4 button on your keyboard.

	hours	wages	Holiday pay		5%
joe	35	$ 21.00	$	735.00	=E4*F2
brenda	22	$ 23.00	$	506.00	
lisa	37	$ 16.00	$	592.00	
Henry	40	$ 22.00	$	880.00	

- Press enter to complete the formula. Select the fill handle on the cell and drag the formula down.

	hours	wages	Holiday pay		5%
joe	35	$ 21.00	$	735.00	$ 36.75
brenda	22	$ 23.00	$	506.00	$ 25.30
lisa	37	$ 16.00	$	592.00	$ 29.60
Henry	40	$ 22.00	$	880.00	$ 44.00

Right Click

- Right clicking on any cell in an Excel Workbook will produce a pop-up menu and a formatting toolbar.

- **Cut**, **Copy** and **Paste** functions are available here.
- The **Insert**, **Delete** and **Clear Contents** are also available.

- **Filter** and **Sort** commands lead to other lists of more specific commands.
- **Insert Comment** – allows you to enter a comment for the cell.
- **Format Cells** opens a dialogue box with numerous options on formatting.
- **Pick from a Drop-down list**- The values must be text and the system will allow you to select from other text values contained in the same column that has no spaces.
- **Name range** opens a dialogue box allowing you to enter a name for the range.
- **Hyperlink** opens a dialogue box allowing you to set up a hyperlink.

Right Click - Row labels

- Right Clicking on row labels produce specific options for the row.

- For Example, we will right click on row number eight in our worksheet.

- From the screen shot below you will sheet that row number eight is highlighted and the pop-up menu is displayed.

- The first sections of commands are similar to the right click on a cell in the worksheet. They are Cut, Copy, Paste and Paste Special.

- The **Insert** command will insert a row above the number eight row that is highlighted. To insert multiple rows, select the number that you would like to insert and right click on one of the selected rows heading number. Select the Insert command and above the top row of the selection the new rows will be placed.

- The **Delete** command will remove that row and all of its contents from the worksheet.

- The **Clear Contents** command will remove the contents but will leave the row and any of its contents as it exists.

- **Format Cells** opens a dialogue box with numerous options on formatting.

- The **Row Height** command lets you specify how tall the rows will appear. When you click on the row height command the following dialogue box will appear. The standard row height is '15' so the necessary adjustments can be made to that number and click O.K.

- The **Hide** command will hide the selected row or rows.

- The **Unhide** command will return hidden rows but the row above and the row below the hidden row must be select before the unhide command will work.

Right Click Column Headings

- Right Clicking on Column headings will produce specific options for the column.

- In our example we will right click on column 'C' in our worksheet.

- From the screen shot below you will sheet that column 'C' is highlighted and the pop-up menu is displayed.

- The first sections of commands are similar to the right click on a cell in the worksheet. They are Cut, Copy, Paste and Paste Special.

- The **Insert** command will insert a column to the left of the column that is highlighted. To insert multiple columns, select the number of columns that you would like to insert and right click on one of the selected column headings. Select the Insert command and to the left of the selection the new columns will be placed.

- The **Delete** command will remove that column and all of its contents from the worksheet.

- The **Clear Contents** command will remove the contents but will leave the column and any of its contents as it exists.

- **Format Cells** opens a dialogue box with numerous options on formatting.
- The **Column Width** command lets you specify how wide the columns will appear. When you click on the column width command the dialogue box will appear. The standard column width is '8.43' so the necessary adjustments can be made to that number and click O.K.

- The **Hide** command will hide the selected column or columns.

- The **Unhide** command will return hidden columns but the columns to the left and the right of the hidden column must be select before the unhide command will work.

Linking screens

- Linking the values from one sheet to another can be achieved by entering the '=' in the destination cell and then selecting the cell from the worksheet desired and pressing enter.

- For example, if you had four worksheets named total, January, February and March.

- You are able to calculate the totals for each of the months on the sheets with the months name on them.

- Then to display the totals on the total sheet you would enter an equal sign = and select the cell from the worksheet required.

- In the two images below, we have the formulas displayed and then the values from these formulas.

	A	B
1	January	=January!E6
2	Febuary	=February!F6
3	March	=March!F6

	A	B
1	January	4214
2	Febuary	3467
3	March	2345

- Note, in the formula, the sheet name is followed by '!'. So that the value in B1 is from the sheet named January and the Cell E6.

Home Tab

Home - Clipboard

- In the clipboard we have the **Cut, Copy, Format Painter** and **Paste** commands.
- A link to a dialogue box is found at the bottom right hand corner.
- **Cut** – select a cell or range of cells – Click the Cut icon and the selection of cells will be removed - available for insertion at some other location.
- **Copy** – select a cell or range of cells – Click the copy icon and a copy of the cells will be available to insert at some other location.
- **Paste** –deposits cut or copied cell in specified location.
- **Format Painter** - Select the cell that has the format you would like to copy. Click the Format Painter paint brush and then click the cell to which you would like to the format.

- Click the arrow leading to the dialogue box.

- The **Clipboard** dialogue box displays all fields that have recently been cut or copied. These fields are available for you to paste.
- Select the destination cell and click on the item in the clipboard display. It will be pasted in the destination.

Home - Font

The Font section of this ribbon allows you to change the type and appearance of your font.

- The top left is the drop-down list to select font type.
- Select the cells and select the type of font from the drop-down list.
- The font will be changed on the selected cells.
- From the toolbar there is a couple of ways to change the size of Font.

- Select the cells and then select the font size from the drop down list.
- Or select the cell and click on the large '**A**' to increase the font size. Each time you click the large '**A**' it will increase by one increment.
- Clicking the small '**A**' will decrease the size of the font by one increment.
- Changing the style of font can be accomplished using these tools.

- Select the desired cells and click **B** for bold, *I* for italic or **U** for underlined.
- The list arrow next to the **U** allows you to select single or double underlined.
- Selecting borders for cells can be accomplished by using the borders button

- Selecting a cell and clicking on the border icon as indicated would create a bottom border for the cell.
- More options for borders can be access by clicking the list arrow.
- The following borders menu will be displayed.

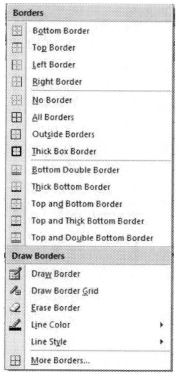

- The Fill colour, which is the background colour of a cell, can be changed by selecting a cell and clicking the fill colour button.

- Next to the fill colour icon is a list arrow. Clicking this list arrow will allow you to select the colour of background colour.

- The font colour icon also has a list arrow that allows you to select the desired colour.

- To change the font colour, select the cells and then select the font colour, and click on the font colour icon.

- The last option that you have from the font section of this ribbon is the link to the dialogue box.

- The link to the dialogue box is located at the bottom right.

- Clicking on this will produce the font form of the format cells dialogue box.

Home - Alignment

- The **Alignment** section of the home ribbon is used to position your data in cells.
- The first set of options is in regard to the vertical alignment.
- Align to the top, align to the centre and align to the bottom of the cell is what is indicated by these three boxes.

- Select the cell and click the vertical format option and the data will be moved to the desired position.
- Horizontal position can be selected by align to the left, align centre and align right buttons.

- To change the data to an angle presentation click the rotate text button .
- From this button there is a list arrow allowing you numerous option.

- Select the text and select the desired formatting options.

- The indent buttons allow you to decrease or increase the Indent within cells.
- The wrap text option allows you to display many lines of text in one cell.

- Select the cell and click the wrap text button
- The **Merge and Center** option allows you to centre a title or heading across a number of columns.

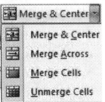

- Enter the text and select the cells that you would like to centre the text across.

	A	B	C	D	E
1	country holiday options				

- Click the **Merge and Center** button and the text will be centered

	A	B	C	D	E
1	country holiday options				

- In addition to the **Merge and Center** command there is a drop down list with additional options available.

Merge & Center

- Merge & Center
- Merge Across
- Merge Cells
- Unmerge Cells

- On the bottom right hand corner of the **Alignment** section of this ribbon, there is a link to the Alignment tab of the format cell dialogue box.

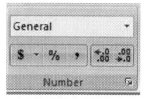

Home - Number

The **Number** section of this ribbon allows you to select how your numbers are formatted.

- Click the list arrow to the right of **General**.
- The following list arrow will be presented.

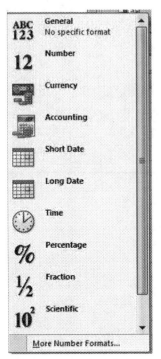

- Selecting a cell and then selecting one of these options will produce the desired number format.
- There are also quick number format options displayed below.

- Selecting a cell and clicking on the dollar sign will format the number to currency. Other currency symbols are available from the drop down list to the right of the dollar.
- Selecting a cell with a number in it and clicking on the % will produce a number displayed as a percentage.
- Clicking on the comma will format large numbers separating thousands.
- Selecting the number of decimal places displayed can be achieved from the following buttons

- Selecting a cell and selecting the left of these buttons will decrease the number of decimal places by rounding the number.
- Selecting a cell and selecting the right of these buttons will increase the number of decimal places.
- On the bottom right hand corner of the **Number** section of this ribbon there is a link to the number tab of the format cells dialogue box.

Home - Styles

The Styles section of this ribbon contains three major sections; conditional formatting, Format as Table and Cell styles.

Conditional Formatting
- Select the range of cells that you would like to conditionally format.

- Clicking the list arrow next to the **Conditional Formatting** icon will produce the following drop down list.

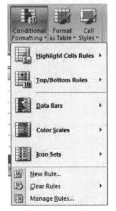

- Select Highlight Cell Rules, for example, will produce an additional menu.

- Clicking on the Greater than rule will produce a dialogue box.

- The first box of this dialogue box is for the value that will determine what values will be highlighted.

- The second box, a drop down list, allows you to select the type of formatting you would like to apply to those cells that meet your criteria.
- To complete this operation click O.K.

Format as a Table

- Select a range of cells and then click the **Format as a Table** icon.
- You will be presented with a variety of formatting options to select from.
- You will be asked to verify your selection. Click **O.K.** and your cells will be formatted as selected.

Cell Styles

- Clicking on the **Cell Styles** icon produces a dialogue box with a variety of cell style options.

- Selecting a cell and then select a style option will format the cell as desired.

Home - Cells

- Clicking the **Insert** will by default, insert a cell or range of cells in the selected location and move the current data down.
- Clicking the list arrow below to the insert will produce options for the insert.

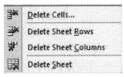

- Clicking the **Delete** icon in the cells section of the ribbon will by default delete the currently select cells and move the data up.
- Clicking the list arrow below to the delete will produce options for the insert.

- **Format** cells provide options for size, visibility, organization of sheets and protection.

Home - Editing

- **AutoSum** will add the numbers that are above the selected cell or to the right or left.
- When you click the **AutoSum** Icon the system will suggest which number it will sum. To accept the suggestion, press enter. The numbers will be summed.
- To the right of the **AutoSum** there is a list arrow.
- Clicking this list arrow will produce a list of commonly used functions.

Σ Sum

Average

Count Numbers

Max

Min

More Functions...

The **Fill** allows you to extend the value to adjacent cells.

- Select a value in a cell and click the Fill icon. You will then be required to select the direction to continue the numbers.
- Select a cell that contains data and click the **Clear** icon.

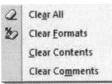

- The system will require you to define what you would like to clear.

- Select a range of cells and click the **Sort & Filter** button to select the type of sort and filter desired.

- The range of cells will be sorted or filtered as requested.

- **Find and Select** icon allows you to locate data as per the drop down list

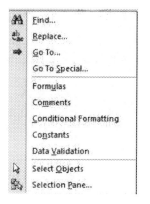

Insert Tab

Insert – Tables

- The **Tables** section of the ribbon gives you options to enter two types of tables: a pre-formatted table and a pivot table.
- *Table* – Clicking on this icon will produce a dialogue box asking where the data is located.
- There is also a check box to indicate whether there are headers for your table.
- The data will be formatted in a pre-existing style table with list arrows on all the column headings.
- *PivotTable* allows you to view data differently. You are able to determine particular details regarding your data from pivot tables.
- For example, we have a list of members for a club as seen in the screen shot below.

	A	B	C	D	E
1	Member ID	gender	area of city	last used	length of Mem
2	1012	male	north	Sep-08	10
3	1013	male	South	Oct-08	13
4	1014	female	west	Nov-08	15
5	1015	male	east	Dec-08	10
6	1016	female	north	Jan-09	13
7	1017	female	South	Feb-09	15
8	1018	male	west	Mar-08	9
9	1019	male	east	Apr-08	3
10	1020	male	north	May-08	9
11	1021	female	South	Jun-08	3
12	1022	male	west	Jul-08	10
13	1023	female	east	Aug-08	13
14	1024	female	north	Sep-08	15
15	1025	male	South	Oct-08	9
16	1026	male	west	Nov-08	3

- We would like to determine how many members of each gender that we have from each area of the city.
- Click Insert Pivot Table and the following dialogue box appear. We will select our table and we will select to place the pivot table on a new worksheet and then click O.K.

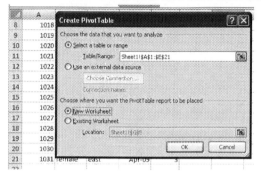

- The PivotTable Field list will be displayed on the new worksheet.

- We will click and drag the 'area of city' to the Column Labels box and then we will drag the 'gender' to the Row Labels.

- To get a count of how many of each gender are in the areas of the city we will also drag areas of the city to Sum of values field.

- We now have a chart displaying how many members of each gender are in each area of the city.

2						
3	Count of area of city	Column Label				
4	Row Labels	e		n s w	Grand Total
5	f			2 3 2 2	9
6	m			3 2 3 3	11
7	Grand Total			5 5 5 5	20
8						

Insert - Illustrations

- The **Picture** icon allows you to select a picture from your computer or your network and insert it in the document.
- The **Clip Art** icon allows you to select clip art from a predesigned selection.
- Clicking on **Shapes** produces an extensive list of shapes to select from.
- Select the desired shape and you will be provided with a crosshair. Click and drag to produce the desired shape.

- Clicking on the **SmartArt** icon produces a dialogue box with option for the type of graphics desired.

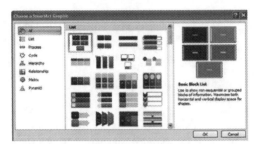

- Select **Hierarchy** and **Horizontal Hierarchy**. Click **O.K**.
- A horizontal hierarch will display on your worksheet.

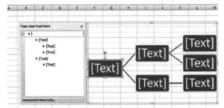

- The Dialogue box on the left is provided for you to enter the desired text for the boxes.
- In addition, displayed on the toolbar is the SmartArt Styles toolbar.

- This toolbar will allow you to change the shape and colour of your graphic.

Insert - Charts

- The **Charts** section of the ribbon allows you to select applicable data and select the type of chart that you would like created.
- For example, we have entered the temperatures for the first twelve days of January. We will select the data that has been entered.

Date	Temp
1-Jan	5
2-Jan	2
3-Jan	-1
4-Jan	6
5-Jan	4
6-Jan	3
7-Jan	4
8-Jan	-2
9-Jan	5
10-Jan	4
11-Jan	3
12-Jan	2

- Select the **Line chart** icon.
- We will be presented with the following options. We will select the single line option.

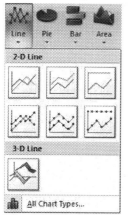

- The single line chart produces the following chart.

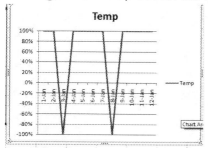

- If undecided on the type of chart, there is a link on the bottom right hand corner of the Charts section to a dialogue box that will help you in the selection.

Insert - Links

The **Hyperlink** icon not only allows you to link to web pages and e-mails but it allows you to create a link to other places in the document or other documents on your computer.

- Click the **Hyperlink** icon.
- The following dialogue box will be displayed.

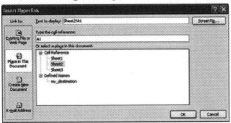

- You will notice that the different types of link options are displayed on the left side of the dialogue box.
- By selecting Place in This Document, we receive a list of the sheet names plus any named cells or ranges.
- Select my_destination .
- The result will be my_destination displayed as a hyperlink that we send you directly to the range of that name when clicked.

Insert - Text

Any of the icons that are displayed in the **Text** section of the ribbon will be inserted but will not be considered part of the work sheet. That is they will not be sorted or used in calculations.

- Clicking on the **Textbox** icon will produce a cross hare allowing you to draw a textbox for your needs.
- Click the cross and hold the click and drag it diagonally to construct the size of textbox that you desire.
- Once the textbox is constructed you will be able to enter text, resize the box using the fill handles or drag it to a new location using the crossed arrows when your cursor is over the borders of the textbox.
- Clicking the **Header** & **Footer** icon will produce the Header & Footer Tools to be displayed.

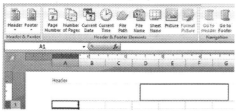

- Clicking on the **Header or Footer** icon in the Header & Footer section of this new toolbar will give you suggestions for the contents of the header and footer.
- The icons in the Header & Footer Elements section are clear as to what information they will automatically add to your header of footer. For example, Clicking Page number will enter the page number and if you desire the number of pages you would key the 'of 'and click the Number of pages icon.
- The navigation portion of this ribbon will allow you to switch between the header and the footer.
- The **Options** section allows you to select, for example, different first page.

Page Layout Tab

Page Layout -Themes

- Selecting **Themes** from the Themes section of this ribbon allows you to select a predetermined combination of colours, fonts and effects for your document.
- Click the **Themes** icon, a drop down menu of theme will be presented for you to select from.
  The icons for Colors, Fonts and Effects allow you to select each of these features individually.

Page Layout - Page Setup

- Click on the **Margin** icon on the Page Setup section of the page layout section of this ribbon.
- This will produce three standard options; Normal, Wide and Narrow. There is also a custom margin option.
- The **Orientation** icon when clicked on will display two options; Landscape and Portrait.
- The **Size** icon allows you to select from a wide variety of paper sizes.
- The **Breaks** icon allows you to enter or remove page breaks.
- Clicking on the **Background** icon allows you to select a file such as a picture to display on the background of your worksheet.

- The **Print Titles** allows you to select the rows and columns that you would like to have printed on each page.

- There is also an arrow at the bottom right hand of this section that leades to the Page Setup dialogue box.

Page Layout - Scale to Fit

The scale to Fit allows you to determine how much information will appear on your printed page.

- Next to each of the dimensions is a drop down list.

- The default for these is automatic which will display standard size sheets.

- The drop down allows you to select the amount of data interims of pages. See graphic below.

- The **Scale** option allows you to increase or decrease the size of your data to suit your needs.

- There is also an arrow at the bottom right hand of this section that leades to the **Page Setup** dialogue box.

Page Layout - Sheet Options

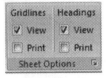

The sheet options allows you select how your document is viewed and printed.

- **Gridlines** is the first option. You are able to select to view them on your screan and, or to print them on your document.

- **Headings** is the second options. Headings referes to the column headings i.e. A, B, C.

- Your are able to select whether they are view on your screen and, or if they are printed on your document

- There is also an arrow at the bottom right hand of this section that leades to the Page Setup dialogue box.

Page Layout - Arrange

The Arrange section of this ribbon allows you to manipulate graphics to achieve the desired result.

- **Bring to Front** allows you move one graphic in front of another.

- **Send to back** allows you to move one graphic behind another.

- The **Selection Pane** lists your graphics on a panel on the side. The selection pane allows you to select, show or hide your graphics.

- The **Align** icon gives you options to aligning your graphics.

- All the graphics that you want to align must be selected and then click the Align option.

- The align options will be displayed in a drop down list. Select the align option that you desire.

- The **Group** option allows you to select two or more graphics and group them. This means that they will acts as one unit.

- They can be moved or changed as one unit.

- The **Rotate** icon allows you to change the orientation of a graphic.

- Select the graphic and click the rotate option. The different rotate options will be displayed.

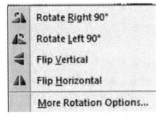

Formulas Tab

Formulas - Insert Function

- Clicking on the insert function icon will produce the following dialogue box.

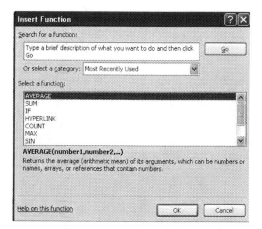

- This dialogue box designed to aid you in selecting the correct function for your needs.

Formulas - Function Library

- The function library has all the functions divided by categories.

- If you have an idea what type of function you are looking for this will narrow down the search.

Formulas - Defined Names

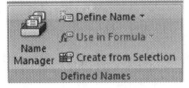

- The **Defined Names** section of the ribbon allows you to manage named cells or ranges.

- Select a cell or range of cells and click on **Define Name** icon.

- The following dialogue box will be displayed allowing you to name the range of cells.

- The **Scope** drop down from this dialogue box allows you to indicate whether you would like this range to be valid for this workbook or for an individual sheet.

- Enter the name for the range and click **O.K.**

- The **Name Manger** lists all your named ranges and their locations.

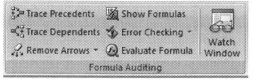

- The Use in Formula icon allows you to use named ranges in formula.

Formulas - Formula Auditing

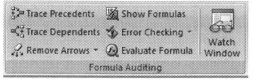

- Clicking the **Trace Precedents** icon will produce arrows showing what cells are related by formula to the value of this cell.

- Arrows will be displayed linking this cell to the cells that result in this cells value.

widget cost	price	profit	est. sales	net profit
$ 5.50	$ 11.50	$ 6.00	3000	$18,000.00
$ 5.50	$ 13.00	$ 7.50	3000	$22,500.00

- The **Trace Dependents** icon will indicate the cells that are dependent on the value of this cell.

- They also will be indicated by arrow drawn on the cells.

- The **Remove Arrows** icon will remove the arrows drawn with Trace Dependents and/or Trace Precedents.

- The **Show Formula** icon will display the formula instead of the value on the entire sheet.

widget cost	price	profit	est. sales	net profit
5.5	11.5	=O4-C4	3000	=E4*F4
5.5	13	=O5-C5	3000	=E5*F5
5.5	15	=O6-C6	3000	=E6*F6
5.5	18	=O7-C7	3000	=E7*F7

- The Show Formula icon acts like a toggle switch. To replace the formulas with values click the Show Formula icon again.

- The **Trace Error** icon gives you a method to check and repair errors that occur on your worksheet.

- The **Evaluate Formula** icon will open a dialogue box that will evaluate the formula step by step.

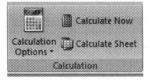

- Every time the evaluate button is clicked the value of a separate part of the equation is displayed.

Formulas - Calculation

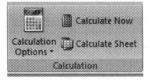

- In Excel formulas are calculated automatically when a value is entered or changed.

- **Calculation Options** allows you to change the calculation times.

- **Automatic** is set by default.

- Selecting **Manual** calculations will make it necessary to use the other option s on this section of the ribbon.

- The **Calculate Now** option will calculate the whole workbook.

- The **Calculate Sheet** option will only calculate the current sheet.

Data Tab

Data - Get External Data

- The **From Access** icon will open your documents, listing only Access files.

- Select the name of the file and the following dialogue box will be displayed that will enquire how you would like the data displayed.

- Click **O.K.** and the data from the Access table will be imported to your worksheet.

- The **From the Web** icon will open Web Query at your home page. You are able to type in the web address of the page you desire in the Address bar.

- There are arrows indicating suitable table to import.

- Click on selected arrow and the table will be selected and then click on the Import Button.

- Another dialogue box will be displayed enquiring where you want the data placed.

- Click **O.K** and the data will be imported.

- The **Data from Text** icon will open your documents listings searching for text files.

- When the file is selected a series of text import wizard screens will be displayed.

- Follow the instructions on each of the three screens and the data will be imported.

- Clicking **From Other Sources** icon will produce a list of other sources that data can be imported from

  - **From SQL Server** connects to a SQL Server table
  - **From Analysis Serves** connects to a SQL Analysis Server

- **From XML Data Import** connects a XML file to Excel
- **From Data Connection Wizard** opens a wizard that guides step by step to connect to external data
- **From Microsoft Query** opens a wizard that will guide you through accessing data from a query either on your computer or on your network.
- The **Existing Connections** icon will open a dialogue box displaying all existing connections.

Data - Connections

- The **Refresh All** icon will update all information that is being received through data connections.

- The **Connections** icon will produce a dialogue box that list all the connections and additional options with these connections.

- The **Properties** icon will produce a dialogue box listing the properties of the external data when the connection is open.

External Data Properties

Connection

Name: Database11

Data formatting and layout

☐ Include row numbers ☑ Preserve column sort/filter/layout
☑ Adjust column width ☑ Preserve cell formatting

If the number of rows in the data range changes upon refresh:
 ⦿ Insert cells for new data, delete unused cells
 ○ Insert entire rows for new data, clear unused cells
 ○ Overwrite existing cells with new data, clear unused cells

[OK] [Cancel]

- The **Edit links** icon allows you to update any connection associated with this file.

Data - Sort and Filter

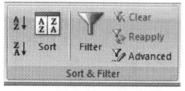

- Select a row or column of data and click on the **A to Z Sort** icon. It will produce a dialogue box inquiring if you would like to expand the sort or continue with the selection.

- Select the option that you desire and click on sort. Your data will be sorted.

- Select a row or column of data and click on the **Z to A Sort** icon. It will produce a dialogue box inquiring if you would like to expand the sort or continue with the selection.

- Select the option that you desire and click on sort. Your data will be sorted.

- The **Sort icon** will produce a Sort Dialogue box which will allow adding options to your sort and sort data.

- Selecting a range of data and then clicking on the **Filter** icon results in a list arrow displayed next to the list of values.

- Clicking the list arrow will result in the following dialogue box to be presented.

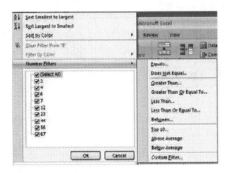

- You are able to filter by the relationship to a value i.e. greater than, less than. You are also able to filter by a specific number or group of numbers.

- In our example we will select the column heading 'net profit' and then click on the filter icon. The list arrows will appear next to the column headings.

ID	pri	profit	est# sal	net profit
2	11.5	6	3000	18000
3	13	7.5	3000	22500
4	15	9.5	3000	28500
5	16	10.5	3000	31500
6	18	12.5	3000	37500

- Clicking the list arrow on the column heading 'net profit'. The following dialogue box is displayed.

We will select the value '22500' and click O.K. The result will be displayed.

ID ▼	pri ▼	profit ▼	est# sal ▼	net profit ☑
3	13	7.5	3000	22500

- Now that the filter has been run, the **Clear** icon becomes active

- Clicking the **Clear** icon will return the data to its original form.

- The **Reapply** icon will run the filter again. If your data has not changed this command will have no effect. If data has changed in your filtered list it will be reflected with the reapply.

- The **Advanced** icon will produce a dialogue box.

- If a previous filter has not been select Excel will estimate the area that you would like to filter in **List Range**.

- You are required to select the **Criteria Range**. Click the Unique records only to filter the list and click O.K.

Data - Data tools

- The **Text to Column** icon divides the data from one column into separate columns. An example of this would be if the first name and last name were entered in the same cell.

- Select the cells that have the names in them.

- Click on the **Text to Column** icon.

- The following dialogue box will be presented.

- Follow the series of dialogue boxes and enter whether the data is separated by commas or spaces for example.

- The data will be separated into multiple columns.

joe	brown
linda	miller
fred	smith

- The **Remove Duplicates** allows you to remove duplicate data from columns or rows

- Select the columns or rows that contain duplicate data.

- Click the Remove Duplicates icon and the following dialogue box will be displayed.

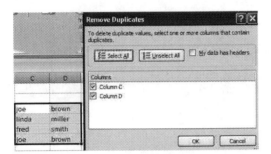

- Confirm the data displayed and click O.K.

- Excel will inform you how many duplicates are remove and how many unique values are present. Click O.K.

- **Data Validation** allows you to specify what type of data appears in a cell or range of cells.

- Select a cell or ranges of cells and Click the Data Validation icon.

- When the icon is clicked the following dialogue box will be displayed.

- When the dialogue box is displayed, you will notice that for the cells selected, it will allow any value.

- Click the list arrow next to "Any value" and the following set of criteria are displayed.

```
Any value                    ▼
Any value
Whole number
Decimal
List
Date
Time
Text length
Custom
```

- For example, select date.

- The next dialogue box will allow you to select the parameters of the date that is to be entered in this cell or range of cells

```
Data Validation                    ? X

Settings   Input Message   Error Alert

Validation criteria
  Allow:
  [Date            ▼]   ☑ Ignore blank
  Data:
  [between         ▼]
  Start date:
  [                    ] 📷
  End date:
  [                    ] 📷

  ☐ Apply these changes to all other cells with the same settings

[Clear All]            [ OK ]   [ Cancel ]
```

- The dates can be between dates, before a certain date, or after a date.

- Also in this dialogue box you are able to enter an input message reminding them of the criteria for data in this cell and you are also able to compose your own error message if the criteria are not followed.

Drop down lists

- To create a drop-down list selects the Data tab and Data validation from the Ribbon.
- The following dialogue box will be displayed

- Under Allow: from the drop down list select **List**.
- In the Source field that is now displayed key in the values that you would like to have in your list separated by a comma.

- When complete, Click **O.K**.
- The cell will appear with a list arrow. Click that arrow will display the values entered.

- The **Consolidate** icon allows you to consolidate data on one sheet or a master sheet.

- For example, if you were recording the marks for your students on separate Excel worksheets, Consolidate would allow you to create a master sheet containing the student's final marks.

- There are a number of ways that you can consolidate data. You are able to consolidate by position in the worksheets, you are able to consolidate by category by using the same row headings and column headings and finally you are able to consolidate data using a formula.

  - **Consolidate using a formula** can be accomplished by selecting your data from multiple sheets for your formula.

  - For example, we would like to calculate the grand total from two sheets. On sheet 1 we will enter the label Grand Total in cell A1 and in cell B1 we will begin the formula with an equal sign =.

  - Now we will click on sheet2 and select cell C4 to capture the total. Next we will enter + and we will click on sheet3 and select cell C4 to capture the other total. Press enter.

- The value will be calculated. In the screen shot below view the resulting formula. Notice by selecting the cells on different worksheets, the sheet reference is automatically added to the worksheet.

	A	B
1	Grand total	=Sheet2!C4+Sheet3!C4

- Clicking the **What If Analysis** icon will produce the following drop down list.

Scenario Manager...
Goal Seek...
Data Table...

- The **Scenario Manager** allows you to determine what the end result of a calculation would be it values are changed.

- For example, if you are trying to determine a price for a product.

- We are manufacturing widgets and below we have initial estimates for cost and price.

widget cost	price	profit	est. sales	net profit
$ 5.50	$ 11.50	$ 6.00	3000	$18,000.00

- We would like to see what the net profit would be if the price was higher.

- Select the cell that contains the value that you would like to change. Click **What-If-Analysis** and **Scenario Manager**.

- Click **Add** on the resulting dialogue box to start the scenario process.

- In the next dialogue box we will name the scenario **Price** and **D4** is the cell where the price is located. Click **O.K.**

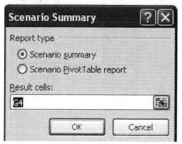

Add Scenario

Scenario name:
Price

Changing cells:
D4

Ctrl+click cells to select non-adjacent changing cells.

Comment:

Protection
☑ Prevent changes
☐ Hide

OK   Cancel

- In the next dialogue box that appears we will enter the price **19.99** and click **O.K.**

Scenario Values

Enter values for each of the changing cells.
1:    D4   19.99

OK   Cancel

- You will be returned to the Scenario manager where you will click Summary and the following dialogue box will be displayed.

Scenario Summary

Report type
◉ Scenario summary
○ Scenario PivotTable report

Result cells:

OK   Cancel

- Select **Scenario summary** and click **O.k.**

- A new sheet will be added to your workbook displaying the following information.

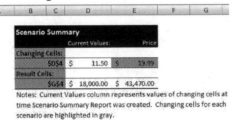

- With the **Goal Seek** option we have another method of determining a price objective in our example.

- Using our widget example we will select the cell that contains the net profit value and we will then select **What-if Analysis** and then **Goal Seek**.

- In the dialogue box we will enter in the **To Value:** field 30,000 and for the **By changing cell:** we will select the cell that contains the price. Click **O.K.**

- Excel will calculate a solution as displayed below. If the solution is acceptable click **O.K.** and if not click **Cancel**.

- **Data Table** is designed to try different values in the same formula.

- For example, we will enter the table below.

	A	B
1	est. sales	3000
2	profit	$ 6.00
3	increase	0
4	profit	$18,000.00

- We have estimated our sales of widgets to be 3000 with six dollars per widget profit. To calculate our total profit we multiplied B1 * B2.

- With a data table we will calculate what our total profit will be if we increased our per widget profit.

- In cells C3 to E3 we will enter increase profits and Select cells as per the screen shot below.

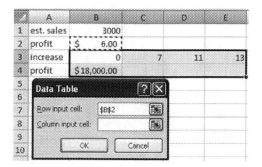

- Click on Data table and in the resulting dialogue box in the row input cell (our replacement values appear in a row) we will select B2 as the value that is changing.

- Click **O.K**. and the profits will be calculated.

	A	B	C	D	E
1	est. sales	3000			
2	profit	$ 6.00			
3	increase	0	7	11	13
4	profit	$18,000.00	21000	33000	39000

Data - Outline

- The **Group** function allows you show and hide details of data as necessary.

- For example, we have our sales data listed by region.

3		
4	Sales 2008	
5	North	$12,560.00
6	South	$ 7,894.00
7	East	$ 9,236.00
8	West	$11,456.00
9	Total Sales	$41,146.00
10		

- We will select the regions i.e. North, South, East and West, and click the **Group** icon.

- We will confirm that we would like to group the rows and click O.K.

- The result will be the data displayed with a minus sign next to the grouped data allowing you to hide details.

	4	Sales 2008	
	5	North	$12,560.00
	6	South	$ 7,894.00
	7	East	$ 9,236.00
	8	West	$11,456.00
−	9	Total Sales	$41,146.00
	10		

- Clicking on the minus sign will hide the details and leave a plus sign indicating that there are more details available by clicking on the plus.

	3		
	4	Sales 2008	
+	9	Total Sales	$41,146.00
	10		

- The **Ungroup** icon will remove grouping of data that has previously been grouped.

- The **Subtotal** icon will automatically calculate subtotals from lists of data.

- In our example we have entered employees, the department and the points that they have earned.

- Ensure that you have column headings for your table.

	A	B	C
1			
2			
3	depart	employee	points
4	Sales	Joe	5000
5	Sales	Tony	3500
6	Sales	Karl	6200
7			
8	Engineering	Bruce	3490
9	Engineering	Keith	7100
10	Engineering	Craig	4500

- Select the table and click the subtotal icon. The following dialogue box will be displayed. We will make the sections as indicated.

- Click O.K. and the subtotals will be added to your data.

1 2 3		A	B	C
	1			
	2			
	3	depart	employee	points
	4	Sales	Joe	5000
	5	Sales	Tony	3500
	6	Sales	Karl	6200
	7	Sales Total		14700
	8			
	9	Engineering	Bruce	3490
	10	Engineering	Keith	7100
	11	Engineering	Craig	4500
	12	Engineering Total		15090
	13	Grand Total		29790

- **Show Detail/Hide Detail** With the rows or columns selected, they will expand or collapse the all of the grouping

Review Tab

Review - Proofing

- The **Spelling** icon will check the spelling of the words in the worksheet.

- The **Research** icon allows you to search through reference guides such as dictionaries and encyclopedias.

- We have clicked the icon Research after selecting the word install.

- The Research dialogue box is displayed and the list arrow is clicked to display the list of resources.

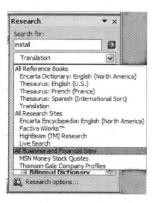

- The **Thesaurus** icon references a thesaurus to suggest words with similar meanings.

- We have clicked the thesaurus icon with the word install selected. The following dialogue box is displayed.

- The **Translate** icon allows you to select a language to which you would like the word translated.

- We have selected the word Today and click the translate icon.

- The following dialogue box is displayed and the list arrow has been click to display the language option available to you.

Review - Comments

- **Add Comment/Edit Comment** allows you to add or edit a comment in the desired cell.

- Cells that contain comments will be displayed with a red corner. When you mouse over the cell the comment will be displayed.

- When you have a cell with a comment, clicking **Delete** on the comments section will remove the comment.

- The **Previous** will move you to a cell previous to the current cell that has a comment attached.

- The **Next** will move you to a cell after this one that has a comment attached.

- The **Show All Comments** will make all the comments visible.

- **Show Ink** is for those users using a tablet computer. Ink refers to the annotations that are created with the tablet pen.

Review - Changes

- **Protect Sheet** icon allows you to specify what areas of the worksheet can or cannot be changed.

- Clicking on the **Protect Sheet** icon will produce the following dialogue box.

- The Protect Sheet dialogue box allows you to enter a password and to check of the conditions desired.

- You will notice that this dialogue box refers to **lock and unlocked cells**.

- By default every cell in an Excel workbook is locked when you protect the sheet.

- If you desire to have some cells available to be changed by other users, you must unlock these cells prior to setting protection on the work sheet.

- Select the cell that you would like to have unlocked.

- Right click on the cell and select the **Format Cells** option.

- Click the **Protection** tab at the top of the dialogue box.

- Remove the check mark in front of **Locked** by clicking on it and Click **O.K**.

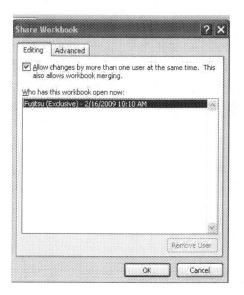

- The **Protect Workbook** icon allows you to enter a password to protect against the movement, addition or deletion of sheets.

- The **Share Workbook** icon allows you have more than one person working on the workbook at the same time.

- The file should be saved to a network location where other people will be able to access the file.

- Click on the Share work and the following dialogue box will be displayed.

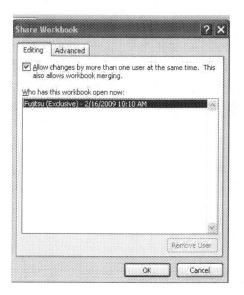

- Click the Allow changes by more...to enable to sharing to take place.

- Once this has been clicked, the Advance tab will now be activated so criteria for the share can be established.

- The **Protect and Share Workbook** icon allows you to track changes made while the workbook is being shared.

- Click the Protect ad Share icon and the following dialogue box will be displayed.

Protect Shared Workbook

Protect workbook for
☑ Sharing with track changes
   This shares your workbook and then prevents change tracking from being removed.
   If desired, a password must be chosen now, prior to sharing the workbook.
   Password (optional):

   [   ]

                              [OK]   [Cancel]

- Clicking the Sharing with track changes check box will allow you to enter a password if desire so that the track changes cannot be turned off.

- The **Allow users to Edit Ranges** icon is another method to unlock cells before the worksheet is protected.

- Select the cell or range of cells you would like to unlock.

- Clicking the Allow Users to Edit Ranges will produce the following dialogue box.

- Click **New** and the range that has been selected will unlock and you will have the option to enter a password.

- The ranges that created here are not to be confused with named ranges created in excel. These ranges are only for the purposes of unlocking the cells and will not appear in any list of named ranges.

- The **Track Changes** allow you to record what changes have occurred to your workbook. This process will also share your workbook.

- The drop down list you are able to select Highlight Changes to start the process or Accept/Reject Changes after changes to the workbook have been completed.

- A dialogue box will be displayed to set the parameters to the track changes i.e. whose changes you want to record, when you want to record this changes and what areas of the workbook to do want to track changes.

- The system will save the document so that it has a point to track changes from.

- When the changes are tracked it will highlight the changes and include a comment on the changes explaining what was done.

View Tab

View - Workbook Views

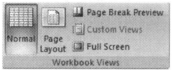

- The **Normal** view icon will return the view in Excel to the view that you have when you first open the file.

- The **Page Layout** view icon will give you a page view similar to print preview with all the features of excel available.

- Page Layout view will present a view of your document similar to how it will look when it is printed. In this view you are also able to add Headers and Footers.

- Column and row header are also available to so that column and row sizes can be adjusted.

	C	D	E	F	G
			Click to add header		
1					
2					
3	widget cost	price	profit	est. sales	net profit
4	$ 5.50	$ 11.50	$ 6.00	3000	$ 18,000.00
5	$ 5.50	$ 13.00	$ 7.50	3000	$ 22,500.00
6	$ 5.50	$ 15.00	$ 9.50	3000	$ 28,500.00
7	$ 5.50	$ 16.00	$ 10.50	3000	$ 31,500.00
8	$ 5.50	$ 18.00	$ 12.50	3000	$ 37,500.00
9	$ 5.50	$ 19.00	$ 13.50	3000	$ 40,500.00
10	$ 5.50	$ 11.50	$ 6.00	2000	$ 12,000.00

Sheet5 Sheet8 Sheet1 Sheet4 Sheet2 Sheet3

- **Page Break Preview** will give you the opportunity to adjust the number of rows and columns that appear on one printed page.

- In the Page Break Preview, the page breaks will be indicated by a blue line. To adjust the size, place your cursor over the blue line and drag out to capture more area or in to decrease the area.

- The **Custom Views** icon allows you to store views that you would like to access again.

- Before you get started save a normal view. Click on Custom views, add and name the view normal.

- Save your worksheet.

- When you have set up a worksheet as you desire, click Custom Views.

- The following dialogue box will be displayed. Click Add to name the view.

- In our example, we have hidden the columns A through C and we have Selected Zoomed to a Selection.

- We will name our view test and we will leave the Print settings and the Hidden rows, columns and filter settings checked.

Add View

Name: test

Include in view
☑ Print settings
☑ Hidden rows, columns and filter settings

OK   Cancel

- Click O.K. and then save your document again.

- Now click Custom Views and Normal and click Show.

- The document will return to its normal settings. Click Custom Views and test.

- The document will return to the special setting we saved.

- The **Full Screens** icon will remove all the icons and toolbars and extend the worksheet the full width of your screen.

- To restore your screen to the normal views. Click the restore icon in the top left hand of your screen.

View – Show/Hide

☑ Ruler   ☑ Formula Bar
☑ Gridlines   ☑ Headings
☐ Message Bar
        Show/Hide

The Show/Hide section of View allows you to different items of the window including:

- Ruler
- Gridlines
- Message Bar
- Formula Bar
- Headings

View – Zoom

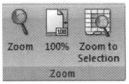

The **Zoom** icon allows you to select different Magnification levels for your window.

- Select the level of magnification that you desire and click O.K. and the windows magnification will be changed.

- The **100 %** icon acts like a toggle switch to return the screen to 100% of the normal value.

- If the magnification of your screen has been changed to a different value, clicking the 100% icon will return it to 100% of the normal value.

- The **Zoom to Selection** will enlarge the cells that are selected. If one cell is selected, then it will increase to up to 400 percent. The increase in size will be proportional to the number of cells that have been selected.

View – Window

- **New Window** icon will open another window of the same sheet.

- The **Arrange All** icon allows you to view all of the active windows at once.

- Clicking the Arrange All icon produces a dialogue box for the selection of how the windows will be arranged.

- Select the desired arrangement and the active windows will be displayed.

- The **Freeze Panes** icon allows you to keep column headings and row headings constant while you scroll through the all the data.

- Click on Freeze Panes icon and you will receive the following drop menu so that you are able to select what area you would like to freeze.

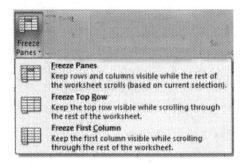

- To unfreeze the pane click on the Freeze Panes icon and unfreeze options will be displayed.

- The **Split** the arbitrarily split the current window.

- To adjust the split, place your cursor over the split bar until a double line with two arrows is displayed.

- Click and drag the split line to the desired location.

- The **Hide** icon will hide the current worksheet.

- The **Unhide** icon will return the hidden worksheet.

- The **View Side by Side** allows you to view different worksheets beside one another.

- Click the **New Window** icon to open another window of the same sheet.

- Select the other sheet by using the sheet tabs at the bottom of the screen.

- Now you will have two different worksheets visible.

- The **Synchronous Scrolling** will enable the scrolling when you have selected view side by side.

- The windows must be side by side so if the position is different drag one of the Excel screen so that horizontal and parallel to the other.

- Click the Synchronous Scrolling and you will be able to scroll and compare the worksheets line by line.

- The **Reset Window Position** icon will return the side by side view back to the normal view of the file.

- **Save Workspace** allows you to save all the windows that you have tiled and aligned so that when you open up the file again they will be set just as you left them.

- The **Switch Windows** icon allows you to switch between all open Excel files.

- Click the Switch Window icon and a drop down list of all open Excel files will be displayed.

- Select the file name and you will be transferred to the other file.

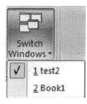

View - Macro

- Recording a Macro can be time saving for worksheets that you use regularly.

- Click on the list arrow below the Macro icon. The Record Macro is the option that we will be discussing here.

- For example, if you were a business that rented medical equipment you would have a spreadsheet that looked similar to the screen shot below.

	A	B	C	D
1	Invoice	customer	doctor	equip
2	10015	David Thompson	Dr. Brown	A480
3	10016	Denise Cox	Dr. Briggs	B398
4	10017	Paul Cooper	Dr. Brown	C225
5	10018	Eric Barber	Dr. Crosby	A480
6	10019	Craig Appelman	Dr. Briggs	C225
7	10020	Diane Weech	Dr. Crosby	B398
8	10021	Donna Hitschfeld	Dr. Briggs	C225
9	10022	David Thompson	Dr. Brown	A480
10	10023	Paul Cooper	Dr. Brown	B398
11	10024	Diane Weech	Dr. Crosby	C225
12	10025	Denise Cox	Dr. Briggs	C225
13	10026	Paul Cooper	Dr. Brown	B398
14	10027	Diane Weech	Dr. Crosby	C225
15	10028	Denise Cox	Dr. Briggs	A480

- We will set up macros to sort the data in two different ways.

- Click on Record Macro. We will name the macro sort_doctor.

Record Macro

Macro name:
sort_doctor

Shortcut key:
Ctrl+ [ ]

Store macro in:
This Workbook

Description:

OK   Cancel

- Select the table and click the data tab and Click the Sort icon.

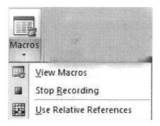

- We will sort by doctor –customer – equipment and click O.K.

- Return to the view menu and click the list arrow below the Macro icon.

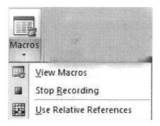

- Click on Stop Recording.

- You will be able to find your macro by clicking on View Macros.

- If you are going to use the macro often it is helpful to attach it to a graphic.

- Click on the Insert tab and Click on Shapes.

- We will select the down facing arrow.

- With the cross hair draw the arrow in the doctor column.

- Right click on the extreme left side of the graphic and this pop-up menu will appear. Select Assign Macro.

- Select the sort_doctor from the list that appears and click O.K.

- Now anytime you would like to run the sort macro all you have to do is click the arrow.

Index